Proverbs 31: A Life of Truth and Grace
By Jessica Mathisen

To Rory, my prince. I'm not the same since you, and I'll be forever grateful.

Table of Contents

Contents

Introduction

Trustworthy, kind, good, hardworking, smart, business-minded, proactive, fit, generous, confident, prepared, crafty, compassionate, wise, caring, godly, diligent, gentle, meek, strong, faithful, and blessed. These are the adjectives that I have written in my Bible next to the passage of Scripture that describes a woman of virtue. Overwhelmed yet?!

When I lived in Mexico, I attended a Calvary Chapel church. Before I moved to Chihuahua, I had never heard of Calvary Chapel churches. However, I soon grew to love this unique body of believers. Calvary Chapel churches study the Bible verse by verse. It is quite powerful when we allow Scripture to just be Scripture and ask the Holy Spirit to speak to us through His word. In this devotional, we will be looking at Proverbs 31:10-31 verse by verse. I hope and pray that the Lord uses His word to encourage you and to challenge you. It is living and active, and when you ask Him to use it to sharpen you, He will most assuredly do so.

We have heard many myths about the Proverbs 31 woman. Many of us may think that she was the perfect woman and had it all, so we might as well not try to match her success. Does this sound like an attitude the Lord wants us to have? May it not be so. The Proverbs 31 woman is "an ideal: a particular example of full-scale virtue and wisdom toward which the faithful are willing to be molded. It is not expected that any one woman will look exactly like this in every respect." {ESV Study Bible footnotes} Sisters, the Lord does not desire for us to strive for an unattainable ideal, but rather to learn from the characteristics of a woman who sought the Lord with every fiber of her being.

The first time I studied the Proverbs 31 woman was about ten years ago. I was a sophomore in high school, and our D-Group (I think that's what we called it back then) went through a study called Virtuous Reality by Vicki Courtney that was intended for college women. I remember being so fascinated with this Proverbs 31 woman, desiring to be made like her and imagining ideals of my future self while completing the Bible study homework each week. As I've grown in the last ten years, the Lord has shown me just how important it is to seek to be found faithful to Him. The Scripture passage in Proverbs 31 is not a checklist for the woman who wants to be found worthy, but rather a set of characteristics to embody only through the power of the Holy Spirit. Let's seek to be known as women who love Him instead of women who take pride in checking off a list of to-dos. He's worthy of our worship in spite of, and perhaps because of, our weaknesses.

As you read through each day, you will be prompted to consider and answer questions that will allow you to think further about that day's reading. You will also be encouraged by words from real Proverbs 31 women who just so happen to be some of my dear friends. I pray you enjoy this study and come to know Jesus more as a result. He loves you so much and longs to be known by you. I love you, friend!

*Note: Maybe you're new to the whole Jesus thing and aren't quite sure what you're in for. That's ok. Jesus longs to know you. Being a Christian isn't about a set of rules or a perfect life. It's about Jesus. Period. God created us to know Him and be known by Him. He wants us to trust Him with all of our lives and walk in relationship with Him. Our sin separates us from God. Sin is anything that does not honor Him. When He created us, He created us to live in perfect fellowship with Him, just like you and your best friend who can hang with each other so easily. Sadly, Adam and Eve wanted to be like God- to have His power- and things got really messed up when they chose to disobey Him in the Garden of Eden. This first sin introduced the whole world to a plethora of bad choices and brought heartache and death. We are dead in our sins and doomed to be separated from Him in hell for eternity if we constantly choose sin over Him. But the good news - the Great News - is that He sent His Son Jesus to pay the penalty we owe Him. He is the only man to live a perfect life and honor God with every fiber of His being, and because He died an awful death on the cross and rose from the grave three days later, we can have life with Him and His Father when we place our faith in Him. I pray that you know Him, and if you don't, let's chat. I would be overjoyed to talk with you more about God's perfect love. Email me at jess56@gmail.com.

Day 1: More Precious than Jewels

An excellent wife who can find? She is far more
precious than jewels.
-Proverbs 31:10

One thing that you may not know about this special passage of Scripture that we now refer to as the "Proverbs 31 woman" is that it is an acrostic. This part of the Bible was written in Hebrew, and my footnotes say that it was most likely written as an alphabet acrostic in order to "show that this woman's character runs the whole range of excellence." {ESV Study Bible} The successive use of the alphabet's letters would have been something that the original readers would immediately notice. They understood the Scriptures and knew that each word was intentional and useful for teaching.
{2 Timothy 3:16}

The verse describes this woman first and foremost as an excellent wife. When we read this verse, we are not to become frustrated, thinking that we cannot live up to this woman, but rather encouraged to pursue the virtues of one incredible gal. As a self-proclaimed grammar nerd, the adjectives are what jump out to me here. Excellent means outstanding, a cut above the rest. Precious describes something that is of great value. Another definition states that it is a "term of address used to a beloved person." Sisters, regardless of our marital status, we are precious in the sight of the Lord. He made us and loves us. Every day He is in the process of redeeming us. He wants us to know that when we seek Him above all else, we are made more and more like Him.

In this you rejoice, though now for a while, if necessary, you have been grieved by various trials, so that the tested genuineness of your faith-more precious than gold that perishes though it is tested by fire-may be found to result in praise and glory and honor at the revelation of Jesus Christ.
- 1 Peter 1:6-7

For my single and married friends alike, know that whatever you are going through right now is of use to the Father. He can use anything to make us precious like jewels. He gives treasures out of darkness {Isaiah 45:3} and works to redeem even the ugliest of paths. The band Gungor's song "Beautiful Things" proclaims, "You [God] make beautiful things; You make beautiful things out of the dust; You make beautiful things; You make beautiful things out of us." So whether you feel excellent or precious, know that He is working on your behalf to do what only He can do-bring good out of the mess. We often do not feel excellent or precious, because when life takes a different turn, we doubt the goodness of who God is. But His path is always better-even when it is marked by fire. A genuine gold is only proved genuine when the fire strips away the impurities and reveals the true beauty of the metal. So our faith is only proved genuine when the Lord takes away all things that keep us from Him.

"Womanhood is a beautiful and powerful thing. Don't be afraid of it, don't reject it, and find your purpose in it. Only then will you be fulfilled."

-Lisa Rafferty

Walking in Truth

Are you willing to go through the fire and be proved genuine before Him?

Do you want to be made into that excellent and precious woman? Ask the Lord to give you His desires for your life.

Day 2: The Value of Trust

The heart of her husband trusts in her, and he will have no lack of gain. - Proverbs 31:11

When I was younger, I had a problem with lying. It started out with "white lies" and quickly escalated to tales I weaved about pretty big things. I had a hard time keeping up with my stories and often felt trapped. It was as though I had convinced myself that my lies were actually the truth. Each time I lied, my heart would just sink inside me, knowing that I was not staying true to who I knew I was in Christ. It took years for me to be able to regain the trust of my parents again.

Today's verse is heavy with an important truth. Trust is the very foundation of any healthy relationship. When I taught elementary school, my heart would break when I had students who struggled with honesty, as I could truly empathize. Most liars lie out of fear- I know it well. Trust is a key element to becoming a Proverbs 31 woman. Without trust, we cannot come to God with our hearts, and He cannot change us and renew us. When we put our trust in Him, He transforms us, making us able to trust others and allowing others to trust us, too.

Our deepest fears often lie in the dark places where we've been misunderstood in the past and have now built up walls. The Lord wants something so much greater for us, though. He wants us to love without abandon and know that we can trust others. There is so much intimacy and goodness within relationships where trust is great and love is unconditional. Married friends, I pray that you find this intimate trust within your marriage, and if not, that you pray for reconciliation or vulnerability where it is necessary. Single friends, I pray you get real with the Lord and allow Him to speak into your dark places and ask him to help you build healthy relationships with established trust. He's so good, and He loves to give us good gifts. May we trust Him to do so.

When I think about what it is to be known and walk in complete trust, I think of the story of the woman at the well in John 4:4-42. In a nutshell, Jesus approaches an outcast at a well, and the chains fall down. She places her trust in Him, which moves her to tell others and bring them to Him. To be known by Him frees us to know others. Let's jump into genuine relationship together, ladies.

"Palms up, sister. Literally. Put your knuckles on your knees and your palms up. The spiritual surrender will follow this physical posture. You own nothing you hold. Receive what He gives you, even if it's unexpected. A life of walking with the Holy Spirit is a continual posture of "palms up." Listening and receiving and surrendering."
-Allison Gibbs

Walking in Truth

Do you have relationships in which you are fully known by others?

With whom do you have these relationships?

How can you walk in truth and trust in relationships that point you and others to the Gospel of Jesus Christ?

_____
_____
_____
_____
_____
_____
_____
_____
_____
_____
_____
_____
_____
_____
_____
_____
_____
_____
_____
_____
_____
_____
_____
_____
_____
_____
_____
_____
_____
_____

Day 3: A Woman Who Does Good

She does him good, and not harm, all the days of her life.
- Proverbs 31: 11

Just what exactly does it mean to be good? It is a word we throw around frequently, as we use it to describe food, music, television, and behavior. However, the actual definition may surprise you, as it did me. The noun form of good is defined as 1) that which is morally right; righteousness, and 2) a benefit or advantage to someone or something.

When I read this verse in the light of the definition of what is good, my understanding deepens, and the word takes on a new meaning. To do good for someone means that you act on their behalf. As a former teacher, I saw my kids in various lights as they interacted with one another through each day. I sometimes grew so frustrated when they did not get along with one another and treat each other with kindness. Other times I was so encouraged as I watched them get out of each other's way and consider one another. To do good to another means that we forget about our own needs and recognize the needs of the other. It means that we allow their needs to supersede ours.

Do nothing from selfish ambition or conceit, but in humility count others more significant than yourselves. Let each of you look not only to his own interests, but also to the interests of others. Philippians 2:3-4

This consideration of others' needs is not natural for us. We want to please ourselves. We want to look out for our own interests. But a woman who does good does not only takes care of herself, but of others. A woman who takes care of others is valuable because she takes the time to get out of her own world in order to step into another's world. Isn't that someone you'd like to be? In order to be that woman, we've got to trust God to be in us what we cannot be. Only He can open our eyes to the needs of others around us. Let's trust Him to do so.

"If I choose to be generous even when I don't feel generous, God is able to work through me and change others in ways that I would never have expected. God needs me to be open to anything he puts in my path, and I have to be willing and bold enough to take part in what He is doing."
-Hannah Hussain

Walking in Truth

Do you live in a way that allows others to be first?

Do you want to see others succeed and celebrate their good? Ask the Lord to help you want good for others. {See Romans 12:15}

What are a couple ways you could weave more "good" into your daily life?

_____
_____
_____
_____
_____
_____
_____
_____
_____
_____
_____
_____
_____
_____
_____
_____
_____
_____
_____
_____
_____
_____
_____
_____
_____
_____
_____

Day 4: Willing Hands

She seeks wool and flax, and works with willing hands.
- Proverbs 31:13

At first glance, you may want to pay attention to the latter portion of Proverbs 31:13. When I read "works with willing hands," I think about work as the labors we endure from nine to five on Monday through Friday. Work is not just what we do to pay the bills, though. Work is labor. It can be chores around the house, rearing children, or the hard work of relationships. To work with willing hands means that we do not complain nor despise our work- even when our job is exceedingly difficult and we think we've got it bad. Instead, we work as unto the Lord, not man.

Each job has aspects that are pleasant and not-so-pleasant. Even your dream job may have parts that you just plain don't like to do. But God says that work is good, and He allows us to work by giving us responsibilities that enable His glory and His good to shine through the earth.

The former portion of the verse says that this woman "seeks wool and flax." In Biblical times (and now), wool and flax were used as material for clothing. Thus, this woman sought out the materials necessary to make her garments. When the Proverbs 31 woman went to work, she was prepared. We can learn from her example and be prepared each day for the tasks that God has entrusted to us. As I dig deeper and learn about this verse, my temptation is to think, "That's great for her, but I can't sew a button on a pair of pants." And while I believe that the words of the Bible are all literally true, I also know that we are not called to emulate every word we read in this passage. The characteristic that we must take away from this verse is that of a good work ethic.

As a child, my parents instilled in me the power of a good work ethic. This value is something I am deeply grateful for and want to instill in my future children as well. Those who know the value of hard work are scarce, and yet it is what the Lord requires of us. May we be women who work hard and are not afraid to get our hands dirty.

"I think we are given opportunities to show Christ's love in any and all aspects of our lives. It is our choice if we choose to take those opportunities and flourish. We don't have to "go" anywhere to be influential. Our relationship with God and His love for us is not measured by our success. We don't create a résumé for God to look at for Him to decide if we are "good enough.""
-Teresa Robison

Walking in Truth

How can you allow the Lord to use your everyday routine to bring Him glory?

Do you see your work as a means for you to build the kingdom of God?

What are three positives about the work you do currently, whether it is school, a 9-5, or raising kids?

_____
_____
_____
_____
_____
_____
_____
_____
_____
_____
_____
_____
_____
_____
_____
_____
_____
_____
_____
_____
_____
_____
_____
_____
_____
_____
_____
_____

Day 5: A Nourished Woman

She is like the ships of a merchant; she brings her food from afar.
- Proverbs 31:14

Food is one of my passions. I love to prepare it, eat it, and share it with others. When I read this verse, I think about the ways in which our food is delivered to us today. We have stores with thousands of food items that stock the shelves. There are aisles and aisles of choices. How do we know how to properly nourish our bodies when there are so many books and diet plans that bombard us through the magazines we read and the fads we see on television? Should I be Paleo or vegan? Gluten-free or vegetarian? The choices are endless, and I am not a registered dietitian, nor do I claim to be any kind of professional.

Here's what I know: food was meant to be enjoyed. Our God is an amazing Creator who made thousands of amazing foods that are completely delicious on their own without additives and chemicals. I cannot claim to be an expert nor a perfect example of what it means to nourish yourself well, but I can tell you that I want to be someone who eats to live, instead of living to eat. Oftentimes, I find myself in the latter camp, as I am constantly thinking about the next meal- wondering what I'll make for dinner when I get home as I eat my lunch. You know how it goes.

Eating well can take an obsessive turn if we aren't careful. As women, it is easy for us to rationalize our obsessive behaviors when counting calories or working out too hard, saying that we are "just taking care of ourselves." Hear this, ladies: self-deprecation and starvation are never ways that we take care of our bodies. Yes, we should avoid junk and look for ingredients that will strengthen us and give us vitality. But let's not allow ourselves to slip into the trap laid by the enemy that gives us yet another reason to think less of who Christ made us to be.

I want to be a woman who eats well and nourishes her body so that it is able to more fully complete the will of God. If I am not at my best physically, how will I be able to walk in obedience to what God has for me? Being a Proverbs 31 woman means that I take the time to seek out good food- food that is not only satisfying and tasty, but that can nourish and energize me, giving me the strength I need to fulfill all that God has called me to do with stamina. From a former runner's perspective, I knew I could perform so much better when I ate well than if I scarfed a Chick-fil-A sandwich before a race. You feel me? Let's be women who eat to live by taking care of the temples God has entrusted us with for this life.

"The Father knows and loves you, wherever you are! Look to Him for your identity and security. Knowing who we are as daughters in Christ frees us to better serve and love others because our confidence is ultimately in Him and not in others. "
-Sarah Thompson

Walking in Truth

Are you taking care of yourself by eating well?

What are some baby steps you could take towards physical health?

_____
_____
_____
_____
_____
_____
_____
_____
_____
_____
_____
_____
_____
_____
_____
_____
_____
_____
_____
_____
_____
_____
_____
_____
_____

Day 6: How To Be a Morning Girl

She rises while it is yet night and provides food for her house-hold and portions for her maidens.
-Proverbs 31:15

When I was younger and slept over at a friend's house, no matter how late we stayed up, I was always the first one awake in the morning. Nothing has changed now. I have to be at work at 9:00, and I live about thirty minutes away. Yet I get up between 6:00 and 6:15 each day, and I don't always hate it. In fact, I enjoy it. There is something special about that time when no one else is up. This time is so sacred to me; it is when I am truly alone with the Lord. Psalm 90:14 says, "Satisfy us in the morning with your unfailing love, that we may rejoice and be glad all our days." The Lord truly does satisfy, and the morning is one of the best times to remember that and carry it into the tone that I set for my day.

My parents both modeled what it looks like to spend time with God. My dad is a morning person, whereas my mom is more "10-2." □As I've gotten older, I confess that I enjoy a couple days to sleep in, but the morning is most definitely my favorite time of day. I have learned that there is great worth in spending time with the Lord before facing the day. During the day, there are so many needs to attend to at school. When I get home, I want to veg out and just watch Gilmore Girls on Netflix or lose myself in a book. Then there's Bible study and hanging with my hubs and making dinner and working out and ALL OF THE THINGS. Oh yeah and trying to have friends.

The Proverbs 31 woman recognizes the importance of dedicating her time to the Lord and allowing moments in His presence to set the tone for her day. Robert Murray M'Cheyne said "For every look at self, take ten looks at Christ." When we begin the day with looking into the face of Christ through His living word, we inevitably invite Him in and allow Him to shape our day, and we are better for it. Maybe you're reading this and thinking, "That sounds nice and lovely, but I am a hot mess express that cannot put sentences together before 8 a.m." Ok- God knows that. Start slow. I began with just a few minutes in the morning, but now hate to stop what I've got going to get ready for work. The Lord knows your heart, so talk to Him about it. You'll be glad you did. Set that alarm clock a few minutes earlier for one week, and just watch what He does.

"Every day is a gift from God, He has the blueprint and you follow the directions. "
-Olivia Wolf

Walking in Truth

Do you have a set time that you spend with the Lord?

Can you allow God to have at least the first five minutes of your day and begin it with prayer and some time in the Word? If not in the morning, when will you commit to spend time with God? Give yourself a little extra motivation with a special candle or hot drink that is just for this time.

_____
_____
_____
_____
_____
_____
_____
_____
_____
_____
_____
_____
_____
_____
_____
_____
_____
_____
_____

Resources for your time with Jesus

First 5 app for phones
My Utmost for His Highest by Oswald Chambers
Jesus Calling by Sarah Young
Jesus Today by Sarah Young
She Reads Truth: online Bible reading plans at www.shereadstruth.com
Give Me Jesus journal found at www.lifelivedbeautifully.com
Prayer Journal found at www.valmariepaper.com

Day 7: Mind on My Money, Money on My Mind

She considers a field and buys it; with the fruit of her hands she plants a vineyard.
-Proverbs 31: 16

Let's be honest, stereotypes are stereotypes for a reason. They are grounded in truth and have an element of consistency to them when held up against fact. When I hear the word business, I think of money and numbers and businessmen and things that are oh so scary to me. I think of my father and his sharp mind, quick to figure the best deal.

My father is honestly one of the smartest men I know. We jokingly call him the closet genius. He reads and retains so much information in that brain of his, and he is quite knowledgeable on a myriad of subjects. Daddy, if you're reading, don't let this go to your head. :) As a child, I received a weekly allowance of one dollar. And do you know what I had to do with 10% of that dollar? I had to tithe each Sunday. So for you mathematicians out there, I made ninety cents a week. Big ballin', right?! The importance of tithing taught me that my money is not my own. Everything I have belongs to the Lord, and I have to treat it as such. Now that I make just a smidge more than ninety cents a week, I am sometimes tempted to withhold my tithe. But I have learned that God does so much more with my 90% than I could do with my 100%. The Proverbs 31 woman is not financially frivolous, allowing her money to slip out of her hands, unaware of its destination. Instead, she plans and considers how best to spend the money that she has. She makes investments by planning for the future, and she takes care of her needs before indulging her wants. I wish I could say that I do all of these things. My dad has taught me so much about money, but if I'm being honest, I have to say that I still have so much to learn.

Here are a few quick tips that have helped me stay afloat:

1) When you pay for something using a credit card, pay it off as soon as possible.
2) Try your best to save something every month. Twenty dollars is something!
3) Track your purchases and see where you are spending needlessly. That way, you know where to cut back.
4) Don't feel bad about treating yourself sometimes. (That advice definitely comes from my mom and not my dad. Love you Mama.)
5) Tithe. When you are generous, it comes back around. That is His promise to us. Don't be afraid and hold on to what isn't yours.

"Bring the full tithe into the storehouse, that there may be food in my house. And thereby put me to the test," says the LORD of hosts, "if I will not open the windows of heaven for you and pour down for you a blessing until there is no more need." - Malachi 3:10

"What we- and I include myself in this, because I have been guilty of it as well!- have to do is look back at what God has called us to, and focus not only on doing our jobs and living our lives well, but living in a manner that attracts and points people to Christ."
- Kai Dickson

Walking in Truth

Do you tithe? Why or why not?

How can you honor God with your finances?

_____
_____
_____
_____
_____
_____
_____
_____
_____
_____
_____
_____
_____
_____
_____
_____
_____
_____
_____
_____
_____
_____
_____
_____
_____
_____
_____
_____

Day 8: A Woman of Strength

She dresses herself with strength and makes her arms strong.
- Proverbs 31:17

I love the Scripture for today's look at the Proverbs 31 woman, because it takes us back to what is most important about our appearance. It is not that we are a size two or that we have a thigh gap, but that we are clothed with strength.

As a child, I never played sports. Ever. No soccer or basketball, tennis or horseback riding. When we lived in Indianapolis, I did ballet for a year, but we didn't keep up with it when we moved to Marietta. Sports were never really my thing; my parents did not play sports growing up, and I just never asked to be a part of them. You could find me with my nose in a book. My sister and I loved to ride our bikes and swing on our swing set in the backyard, but when it came to playing with the boys and actually throwing a ball or getting a game going, that was all Lauren. Not I. I was "GG"- Girly Girl, and she was "TB"- Tomboy.

In high school, I found that I loved home videos because they were convenient, but I also loved group fitness classes at the YMCA. Zumba is life-changing, ladies. Fast forward to college, and it seemed like everywhere I looked, people were running. And they liked it. Now, my experience with running was the mile run in middle school and high school. And I loathed it. But when I signed up to take a walking class for my physical education credit, I found that I enjoyed being outside and loved taking in the sights around me while listening to music. The practice calmed me, and I figured that I should make it a part of my life outside of my P.E. class. I began walking to class, foregoing the bus and trekking it around UGA's huge campus. In time, I began to experiment with running. One day I decided that I was going to place a goal before myself and train for a half marathon. Finishing that first race was one of the greatest feelings of my life, and now I've run five of them!

Exercise is not meant to be tortuous, but rather a means of taking care of the bodies that God has entrusted us with for our time here on earth. My preferred means of exercise is walking or running, but I also enjoy Zumba and Pilates. Zumba makes me come alive and makes me feel more beautiful and feminine as I "shake what my mama gave me." Pilates challenges me as I contort into positions that seem like they are meant for pain instead of strength. I find myself praying and asking the Lord to help me keep my eyes on Him as I work on balance and strengthening my core.

The Proverbs 31 woman is not a woman who intimidates others by being an overachiever who bests everyone and makes others look weak. Instead, she is a woman who cares about her body. She understands the importance of fitness, and she seeks to take care of herself by staying active not only for herself, but also for her family and for the wellbeing of those around her.

"Happiness is not the absence of challenge." -Allie Beck

Walking in Truth

How can you get moving today?

What is your favorite way to take care of yourself?

_____
_____
_____
_____
_____
_____
_____
_____
_____
_____
_____
_____
_____
_____
_____
_____
_____
_____
_____
_____
_____
_____
_____
_____
_____
_____

Day 9: A Resourceful Woman

She perceives that her merchandise is profitable. Her lamp does not go out at night. She puts her hands to the distaff, and her hands hold the spindle.
- Proverbs 31:18-19

So this Proverbs 31 woman is basically a boss. She doesn't play games, and she means business. Literally. This pair of verses paints a clear image of a woman who is resourceful and also seeks various avenues in order to help provide for her family. In Christian circles, it is very easy for us to fall into the trap of believing that there is one way for family dynamics to be "healthy" and "right." We can easily think that being a Proverbs 31 woman consists of marrying the perfect man, bearing the perfect children, and maintaining the perfect friendships. But my friends, that thought process simply is not true.

In these verses, we see that this woman contributes to the financial stability of her home. She works hard and uses the fruit of her labor to provide for her family. My desire for children is genuine. As a child, I mistakenly believed that there was one right way to maintain a home. I thought that once a woman married, she must stay home to take care of the children-working was for men. As I've grown and matured, I've seen that there is no formula.

These verses free women from the lies that say you have to choose between a career and a family. Each woman is completely different, created with gifts and abilities unlike any other. God places desires and passions within the hearts of every woman and cultivates them, allowing her to see and believe that she can be used for His kingdom within and outside of the home. The Proverbs 31 woman is not afraid of hard work, and she is also not afraid to go against the grain in order to do what is best not only for her, but also for her family members.

"She desires to embrace all that God has called and purposed for her to do, and is willing to step out in faith, and outside her comfort zones, to answer that call. She is about God's Kingdom work here on earth and investing in things of eternal value."
-Jennifer Brommet

Walking in Truth

Do you believe that there is one right way to make a living?

How can God use your gifts and talents to help others while also providing for your needs?

If you could work one job for the rest of your life, what would it be?

_____
_____
_____
_____
_____
_____
_____
_____
_____
_____
_____
_____
_____
_____
_____
_____
_____
_____
_____
_____
_____
_____
_____
_____
_____
_____
_____
_____

Day 10: A Heart for the Poor

She opens her hand to the poor and reaches out her hands to the needy.
- Proverbs 31:20

I was first introduced to Compassion International in high school at a Dare 2 Share evangelism conference. I remember sitting in the arena, tears flowing down my face as I heard about the extreme poverty many children around the world face on a daily basis- all due to circumstances beyond their control or choosing. A friend and I decided to sponsor a child for a couple years together. When I went to college, I was unable to continue my support. However, the desire to be a part of a child's life was still there.

About five years ago, when I was still living in Mexico, I was reading a friend's blog and saw that she had the opportunity to meet her child that she sponsored through World Vision. I was so moved by what I saw, but was more familiar and comfortable with Compassion International. That day, I went to the Compassion website and chose a sweet little girl who lives in southern Mexico. I chose her because I love the country of Mexico and hoped that one day I might meet her. Unfortunately, her parents chose to discontinue her sponsorship, but I still think of and pray for her often. I now have another little girl from Mexico named Ninbe, and I look forward to beginning correspondence with her soon.

About two years ago, I was reading my daily (in)courage email, and author Emily Freeman wrote about her experience in Uganda. I knew that I would be headed there in a few months, and when I returned, I chose a Ugandan boy to sponsor. He is the sweetest thing, and I love receiving his letters in the mail. What I love about Compassion is that they are so intentional. They communicate well and make it clear that you matter as a sponsor. I am able to write letters to my children and receive letters as well. Periodically, I also receive a letter from the pastor of the local church or the leader of the child development center. When I receive a letter from either one of my children, I am so excited to read about how they've changed and grown. They pray for me, and I pray for them. My desire is to sponsor them as long as I can. My dream is to meet them in person. God has given me a heart for children who are in difficult situations. This is His heart- Jesus wanted the little children to come to Him. (Matthew 19:14) God created each child with a name and a purpose. And His heart is for them to thrive, not just survive. One day, Lord willing, we would love to adopt. For right now, though, we can sponsor these sweet children who live in countries where the Lord has stirred my heart, knowing that because of our little part in their lives, they will go to school and have brighter futures. God's heart is for children to be in families, and when they are able to stay with their families, they are empowered and inspired.

Our money is not our own. The resources we have are given to us for a reason. Would you think about where your 10% or your surplus goes each month? Prayerfully consider sponsoring a child today, and know that your commitment will truly change not only the life of that child, but that of their family and community as well.

"I've seen God bring healing and freedom into my life and the lives of those around me, and seen people fight for God's glory in relationships and their families, repent, and choose love in seemingly impossible circumstances. Even on the hardest days, I know that doing the hard work of pursuing God in community with believers has to be part of what Jesus meant when he talked about bringing God's kingdom to earth."
-Elissa Ewald

Walking in Truth

Are there organizations in your town that help the poor? How can you be a part?

Ask the Lord to open your eyes to opportunities to serve the often forgotten or neglected in your community.

_____

_____

_____

_____

_____

_____

_____

_____

_____

_____

_____

_____

_____

_____

_____

_____

_____

_____

_____

_____

_____

_____

_____

_____

Day 11: What We Wear

She is not afraid of snow for her household, for all her household
are clothed in scarlet. She makes bed coverings for herself; her
clothing is fine linen and purple.
- Proverbs 31:21-22

I am the typical girl- I love shopping and clothes. When we moved into our current home, I was overjoyed that my husband allowed me to have complete domain of our master closet. Growing up, I loved to spend my allowance at Target on a new purse or new shoes. Clothes have just always been something I enjoy. When we think about the way God made us and look at ourselves in light of a creation formed in His image, we must know that God Himself appreciates beauty. He created it and wants to appreciate it in all forms.

The Proverbs 31 woman recognizes that her outward appearance, while not of utmost importance, is something to take pride in and consider. If we are believers, then our bodies are no longer our own, but rather a temple of the Holy Spirit. Our hearts are a home for Him. If our bodies are a home for Him, than we should adorn them in a way that honors Him. I love clothes and putting outfits together. Some women would like to wear yoga pants and a simple tee day in and day out. There is no "right" way to dress. However, I think that these verses encourage us as women to consider the clothing we don each day. Do we dress for each other- to impress and compare? Do we dress for men in order to gain their attention? Do we dress in order to portray a certain status?

Do not let your adorning be external—the braiding of hair and the putting
on of gold jewelry, or the clothing you wear— but let your adorning be the
hidden person of the heart with the imperishable beauty of a gentle and
quiet spirit, which in God's sight is very precious. - 1 Peter 3:3-4

Let's be women who take pride in our outer appearance but understand that our beauty is found in Christ. Yes, clothes are fun- I have a closet full of them and enjoy them very much. But clothing is much more than skin-deep. As we don our favorite cardigan or party dress, let us also remember to dress ourselves in the Spirit by asking the Lord to beautify our hearts and minds.

"His glory and His light shine most radiantly when we clear the stage of our ego and we stand on the platforms in our lives with humility; knowing that there is nothing we can do to deserve to be placed where we are. At that moment, He uses anything and everything for His glory. The beautiful, the ugly, and the broken. That's grace."
-Cortney Norris

Walking in Truth

Does your outward appearance match your inward being?

Who do you dress for- you, others, or a mix of both? How does your outward appearance reflect who God made you to be?

_____
_____
_____
_____
_____
_____
_____
_____
_____
_____
_____
_____
_____
_____
_____
_____
_____
_____
_____
_____
_____
_____
_____
_____
_____
_____
_____
_____

Day 12: God's Plan for Marriage

Her husband is known in the gates when he sits among the elders of the land.
- Proverbs 31:23

Marriage and dating are things that our society has twisted and turned into something completely different than what God intended. Can I get an amen there? Dating is seen by some as a sport in which you conquer whomever you like and move on once you've scored. Marriage is viewed as an arena in which you enter at your own risk and exit when circumstances become too difficult or exacerbating.

But as always, God's ways are higher, and His plans are much different than our own. The Proverbs 31 woman knows this and seeks to live in light of a completely different standard-whether single or married. Marriage is not an accomplishment. It is not for an elite crew of Christians who've "earned it." Marriage is, like any other blessing, a gift from God that is to be used to bring Him glory. Period.

I spent many of my single years pining and hoping for a man who would make everything better and usher me into my fairy tale. And while life is certainly sweet with my husband, he does not complete me or solve every one of my problems. He is, after all, only human. (But a pretty stinkin' great one, just saying.)

A Proverbs 31 woman recognizes the value and sacredness of marriage as an institution between one man and one woman created by God to bring Him glory and further His kingdom on earth. She sees and understands that a man cannot and will not ever complete her.

When seeking a mate, keeping our eyes on Jesus must be paramount to any of the fairy tale dreams we so long to cling to and cherish. In the verse above, there is nothing mentioned of rose bouquets, romantic getaways, and several carat diamond rings. What is noted is the strength of her husband's character. He is a leader amongst distinguished individuals. The verse mentions nothing of a six figure salary or chiseled abs. (Come on ladies, you know you've dreamed of these things!)

Single friends, pray for your future husband. If God has given you the desire to be married, then commit that desire to Him in prayer and trust Him to fulfill it in His timing and in His way. Married friends, look for ways to encourage your husband's strength of character. When times are hard or your nerves are shot, remind yourself of why you fell in love with and married the man you committed yourself to at the altar. And all friends, know that ultimately, Jesus is the satisfier of all your needs.

"Kiss a lot. :) Say "I love you" and "I'm sorry" a lot! Love Jesus most and let Him help you love each other."
-Lyndsey Lovern

Walking in Truth

If you are single, do you pray for your future husband? Do you ask God to give you wisdom and patience for this season?

If you are married, do you value your husband's opinion above that of the Lord?

Do you allow the Holy Spirit to lead and guide you to serve and respect Him daily? Commit your actions to Him.

_____
_____
_____
_____
_____
_____
_____
_____
_____
_____
_____
_____
_____
_____
_____
_____
_____
_____
_____
_____
_____
_____
_____
_____
_____
_____
_____

Day 13: A Good Steward

*She makes linen garments and sells them; she delivers
sashes to the market.*
- Proverbs 31:24

When I think about all of the ways that women are stretching themselves
and running themselves ragged to try to be all things to all people at all
times, it makes me a little dizzy. The world around us is changing at the
speed of light, and there are so many activities and good things that we
can fill our schedule with. Add to that the pressure of making money and
providing for ourselves or our families, and you've got a recipe for some
major stress. But God has another way. He wants us to honor Him with our
financial resources- whether meager or lucrative.

There are myriad ways to make money. God has uniquely gifted each one
of us with talents and passions that, when yielded to Him, bring Him glory
and further His kingdom by encouraging the body of Christ. The verse above
emphasizes that this woman was one who was resourceful- she looked for
ways to make money using her hands and her God-given gifts. Money can
sometimes be a taboo subject in the church- we judge people who have too
much or too little of it. However, we need money in order to function within
our society.

So what do we do with the talents and passions God has given us? Is it ok
to use them to make money and provide for ourselves or our families? I
believe the answer is a resounding YES. God is Jehovah-Jireh, our Provider.
He owns the cattle on a thousand hills, and yet He also gives us resources,
passions, and talents for His glory that can allow us to provide for our needs.
He tells us to look to Him as the giver of all good things, but He also provides
opportunities for us to bless others with our gifts.

If you're wondering how you can serve God and make money by doing what
you love, take it to Him. He does not often give us gifts that are intended to
lie dormant and not be used for Him. When we are good stewards of the gifts
He's given, we bless others, and in turn invite blessing for our homes.

"We have been given specific gifts and specific messages on our hearts to lift up, encourage and come alongside those around us. Every detail of who you are has been outlined by God - the amount of hairs on your head, the lovely curve of your smile, and even the things that make your heart beat faster. You were designed with a purpose in mind to be salt and light to the very world you are living in, and because of Him in you, you already have all that you need to fulfill that!"
-Shaylynn Cherry

Walking in Truth

Do you use your gifts to help you earn money?
Has the Lord provided you a job that allows you to live with your needs met?
If so, praise Him for it!

If you are not currently working, ask for wisdom as you consider your next steps.

_____
_____
_____
_____
_____
_____
_____
_____
_____
_____
_____
_____
_____
_____
_____
_____
_____
_____
_____
_____
_____
_____
_____
_____

Day 14: A Woman of Strength and Dignity

"Strength and dignity are her clothing, and she
laughs at the time to come."
- Proverbs 31:25

Strength: the emotional or mental qualities necessary in dealing with situations or events that are distressing or difficult.

Dignity: the state or quality of being worthy of honor or respect; a sense of pride in oneself; self-respect.

When I think of strength of character and mind, I think of my husband. His quiet strength and peaceful spirit drew me towards him, and these characteristics define him. He is not easily broken down or discouraged. He is also well respected by all who know him, because he is the same person no matter where you find him. Work Rory, Church Rory, Gym Rory, and Home Rory are all the same person- kind, gentle, and patient.

The above characteristics my husband possesses drew me towards him because I so often lack these characteristics in my own life. I am weak. I am a professional complainer and a worry extraordinaire. If there is one thing I have learned from my husband, it is the value of placing my trust in Christ for all things. Literally all things.

It seems nearly impossible for me to sleep through the night these days. My mind reels with thoughts about the day that just passed- how I could have changed things. I drift towards worries of the future- wondering when and how things will happen that I long for and trying to imagine ways to control it all. Bottom line- I'm full of fear instead of faith. The Lord instructs us not to fear 365 times in His word. He knew we would need to be reminded to place our full trust in Him every single day. When we allow ourselves to be consumed with fear and worry, we shortchange ourselves and do not live our best life. John 10:10 says "The thief comes to steal, kill, and destroy, but I have come that they may have life and have it to the full." Satan wants to distract us with worries of the past, present, and future. But this, my friends, is no way to live. It simply is not what God has for us.

The Proverbs 31 woman exhibits strength and dignity because she has clothed herself with Christ. He is what shines through her every action, and she walks with Him so closely that others see Him, too. In a world full of the unexpected around every corner- diagnoses, job losses, terror attacks, financial troubles- Christ is our peace. He gives us joy that can only come from within through the power of His Holy Spirit. We can lay down our troubles and worries and exchange them for His resounding joy. We can look to Him and then look ahead to our future with smiles on our faces, regardless of the forecast, knowing that He is on His throne and that He is always, always, always for us.

"You are enough. Just as you are. Created on purpose and loved so much that God sacrificed His own Son so brokenness in us wouldn't be the end of the story. A God that does that isn't going to forget you somewhere in the trials of your twenties. He's not leaving you to figure it out alone when you mess up. He didn't neglect to make you prettier, smarter or better. You belong to Him. You are enough."
-Janay Boyer

Walking in Truth

Do you ever feel like you have to do it all?

How can the strength of Jesus empower you to rest in Him?

_____
_____
_____
_____
_____
_____
_____
_____
_____
_____
_____
_____
_____
_____
_____
_____
_____
_____
_____
_____
_____
_____
_____
_____
_____
_____
_____

Day 15: You is Kind, You is Smart, You is Important

She opens her mouth with wisdom, and the teaching
of kindness is on her tongue.
- Proverbs 31:26

The title of today's reading is a quote from the movie (and book) entitled The Help. Set in 1960s southern Mississippi, an African American woman is given the responsibility of caring for a sweet Caucasian toddler. Ms. Aibileen cares for little Mae Mobley as though she were her own daughter, speaking words of truth over her every day. The little girl is empowered by her words and finds comfort and strength in her encouragement.

I'm sure you can remember a time in your life when someone encouraged you so specifically that their words still bring a smile to your heart. There are probably other words that have been spoken over you that haunt you and have to be laid down at the foot of the cross more often than you would like to admit. What we say matters. How we use words has the power to give life or to bring death. When we speak life, we build others up, calling them to be who God has created them to be. When we use our words to hurt others, we tear them down, making room for them to doubt who God has created them to be.

James 3:8 says that "no human being can tame the tongue." Apart from the Holy Spirit, our tongues are prone to gossip, grumbling, complaining, and lying. We say what we think and do not give much thought to how it may affect those around us. Some of us may say whatever we like in the name of being "sassy" or "funny." But God takes seriously the use of our words, and He wants us to as well.

The Proverbs 31 woman is said to have wisdom and kindness flow from her mouth. Wisdom and kindness are not qualities that just "come naturally," but rather are cultivated through allowing the Holy Spirit to work in your heart and life as He makes you more like Christ. In order to be more like Christ, we have to know Him. Our head knowledge must become heart knowledge.

How do we know Christ? We spend time with Him in His word. We pray and listen. We seek Him and learn from more seasoned believers who can teach and lead us. So ladies, let's seek to be women who give life with our words and encourage others, coming alongside them and speaking truth with love and grace.

"Telling our testimonies... not only is that a powerful thing, but a great reminder. Take a minute to think of your own testimony. Isn't it incredible how God found you? Whether you were raised in a Christian home and came to know the Lord at three years old, struggled through some crazy trials and came to know the Lord later or anywhere in between: God. Found. You. Rest in that for a moment."
-Stasia Skelton

Walking in Truth

How can you speak truth and life over yourself? Do you treat yourself with kindness?

How can you speak truth and life over others? Are you a grace-giver or a shame-giver?

_____
_____
_____
_____
_____
_____
_____
_____
_____
_____
_____
_____
_____
_____
_____
_____
_____
_____
_____
_____
_____
_____
_____
_____
_____
_____
_____

Day 16: Your Work Life

She looks well to the ways of her household and does
not eat the bread of idleness.
- Proverbs 31:27

When I first arrived to the University of Georgia in the fall of 2006, I was not playing games. I had worked hard for four years to be accepted to my number one college choice, and I knew that if I lost the HOPE scholarship, I was coming home to live with my parents and go to a local school. You could say I had a good dose of motivation to keep my grades up. While I consider myself to be a fairly intelligent individual, I have never been the type of student who could make amazing grades without studying. I always had to work for my grades and was astounded by (and jealous of) those who could fall asleep in class and pass the test with flying colors. A few girls in my dorm noticed my studying habits and commented saying, "Wow, that girl is always studying. She's going to have such good grades!"

Let me just stop and say that I'm a nerd. It's fine; I own it. God's word has a lot to say about our work ethic, though, and He is honored when we honor Him with our work. When we work to the best of our ability, we glorify Him whether we ace the test and make six figures or bomb the test and live on a meager budget. People are watching us. God created each one of us with specific gifts and talents that He wants us to use to honor Him and to point others to Him.

When you stay late to make sure the project is done the right way. When you turn in the assignment early instead of two days late. When you ask for help and attend the study session. When you're honest about each one of your expense reports and go the extra mile to be wise with the company's money. People see, and God cares.

"It's not complicated. I think we like to complicate things, but Jesus was fairly straight forward. He met people where they were at and introduced Himself. He got to know them - though He actually already knew them - and only offered them what they needed. Which was Himself. So I try to get to know people and tell them about my hope."
-Nadine Schroeder

Walking in Truth

Are you a person of character, willing to do the hard work whether people see it or recognize you for it? Do you encourage others in your workplace to do the same?

When is it hard for you to put forth your best effort? How can you allow God to help you honor Him with your work?

_____
_____
_____
_____
_____
_____
_____
_____
_____
_____
_____
_____
_____
_____
_____
_____
_____
_____
_____
_____
_____
_____
_____
_____
_____

Day 17: An Honorable Reputation

Her children rise up and call her blessed; her husband also, and
he praises her: "Many women have done
excellently, but you surpass them all."
- Proverbs 31:28-29

We have been studying the attributes of a woman who seems to have it all. There seems to be no flaw in her. But as we have learned and now know, the opposite is true. This woman is not perfect, nor is she some sort of goddess to whom we pay homage. No, the woman described in this text is rather an example to us of the characteristics the Holy Spirit reveals in us as we grow into the women the Father made us to be.

It is easy to look at the characteristics and actions of the Proverbs 31 woman as a checklist of sorts- one that will tell us what to do to finally "get it together." If we see this passage of Scripture as one that will simply give us another to-do list, we are missing the mark. God sent His Son, Jesus Christ, to help us do away with the checklist mentality. He asks us to trust Him to bear the fruit in our lives; it's not our job. When we look at verses 28-29, we may see the image of our children or husbands (past, present, or future) rising up and blessing us as an impossibility. We are our own worst critics, after all, and we may go through each day berating ourselves, believing we can never get it together and that we will always be just one step away from true happiness, joy, or fulfillment.

Matthew 5:16 says "Let your light shine before men, that they may see your good deeds and praise your Father in heaven." If we look to this passage as a means of gaining praises from others, our motives are rooted in pride, and we are not allowing the Holy Spirit to do the work in us. We will have reverted to the legalism and works-based faith of the Pharisees, who wanted to earn their way to Jesus. Jesus has already given us the freedom to walk with Him and be exactly who He says we are- no one else.

We honor Him with our lives when we allow our actions to point to Him, not ourselves. If the people in our lives call us blessed, let's pray they know that the source of our blessing lies in our heavenly Father.

"God has called us to share His love with those around us right where we are. Seasons change and our location and our spheres of influence change along with them, but there is always purpose to be found and ministry work to be done wherever we are."
-Jenna Simmons

Walking in Truth

Do you care more about your good name than that of your heavenly Father?

Are the blessings in your life distracting you or drawing you closer to the Father, who is the giver of all good things?

_____
_____
_____
_____
_____
_____
_____
_____
_____
_____
_____
_____
_____
_____
_____
_____
_____
_____
_____
_____
_____
_____
_____
_____
_____
_____
_____
_____

Day 18: True Identity

Charm is deceptive, and beauty is fleeting, but a woman who fears the Lord is to be praised. Give her the fruit of her hands, and let her works praise her in the gates.
- Proverbs 31:30-31

For far too long, I wasted time allowing the world to tell me who I was (honestly, I still struggle with this). I searched for my satisfaction in my material possessions, outward appearance, and my relationship status. The problem with looking for love in all the wrong places is that you are never fully satisfied. Material possessions can be lost, damaged, or just get boring after a while. Outward appearance is fleeting and changes over time. Relationships were meant to encourage us in the Lord, not to take His place. Every one of these temporal gifts are but a shadow of who God is, and He created us to find our satisfaction in Him alone. Period.

A woman who fears the Lord recognizes the temptation to find her worth outside of Him but understands the value of knowing God the Father. She understands that there will be days, weeks, and even months of confusion, trial, and frustration. She also bases her worth and joy on the Word, not the world. When chaos ensues, she runs to the arms of her Father, knowing that He hears her cry.

The problem with attempting to find satisfaction outside of Christ is that it will always leave you wanting more. Everything in our lives is subject to change, and the only certainty we have is Christ. He alone is our fortress and the Rock to which we can hold when all else fades away. Because the Proverbs 31 woman recognizes this truth, her hope lies in Christ, and her life is set apart from others. Others are encouraged by her life and seek the truth because of the light that shines through her.

When we allow the Holy Spirit to work in our hearts, we bear fruit as a result of our trust in Him. We don't have to try to have it all together or do everything to the impossible standard of perfection. We just let Him be Him in us. And when we do, we will see the fruit of our hands, and our works will be recognized as Christ's love shines through us.

"We go to great lengths to please ourselves, to protect our own well-being (emotional and physical), and to prop up our own esteem. So the lesson I'd love to see us learn? To die to ourselves and live to Christ. And to enjoy every day forever the incomprehensible reality of God's immeasurable love!"
-Suzanne Chambers

Walking in Truth

Where do you run when you are chasing satisfaction?

Do you allow the Lord to define you and tell you who you are- in Him? Take a minute right now to pray and ask the Lord to help you see yourself as He does.

_____

_____

_____

_____

_____

_____

_____

_____

_____

_____

_____

_____

_____

_____

_____

_____

_____

_____

_____

_____

_____

_____

_____

_____

_____

_____

_____

_____

Conclusion

Where does your identity lie? Where is your hope? Are you asking the world to tell you who you are, or are you looking to Christ? A woman who fears the Lord honors Him in her actions, speech, thoughts, and habits. She asks the Holy Spirit to envelop her being, inviting Him into every aspect of her life. In today's world, it is increasingly difficult to be found steadfast or faithful in any aspect of life. People quit before they truly begin. Husbands and wives give up on one another and forsake their vows. Friends walk away from one another at the slightest sign of conflict.

The Proverbs 31 woman is a woman of steadfast love, faithfulness, and joy. She invites others to walk with her alongside her journey with the Lord, and she is not afraid to look a little different from those around her. The mainstream culture may not often understand her choices, and she may sometimes be seen as one who takes Jesus "a little too seriously." But within her heart, she is fueled by a quiet inner strength that will not be overtaken by the lies or demands of the world. She is encouraged by the community of believers with whom she surrounds herself, and she allows the Lord to gently correct, lead, and guide her footsteps. Her words are those of kindness and grace, and her arms and home are always open.

We've looked at the Proverbs 31 woman as a Biblical ideal that teaches us about true womanhood. Let's allow the Holy Spirit to show us where He still wants to grow and change us.

Lord, thank you so much for the woman reading this study. Thank you for creating her in Your image and for making a perfect plan for her life. Thank you for allowing her to learn more about You through Your word. Please reveal Yourself to her and continue to lead and guide her as she seeks to be more like You.

"Remember Whose you are. Remember who you are. Even though life can be difficult at times, God is there to walk with you.
- Cathy Miller / my mama :)

Walking in Truth

What did you think about the Proverbs 31 woman before beginning this study? How has the Lord changed your idea of who she is?

In what areas of your life do you need the Lord to stir things up a bit? How can you allow the Spirit to lead and guide you?

_____
_____
_____
_____
_____
_____
_____
_____
_____
_____
_____
_____
_____
_____
_____
_____
_____
_____
_____
_____
_____
_____
_____
_____
_____
_____
_____
_____

Further Reading and Study

Money

Dave Ramsey's Complete Guide to Money: The Handbook of Financial Peace University by Dave Ramsey

Identity

True Identity: Do you know WHO and WHOSE you really are? By Jennifer Brommet
Wild and Free: A Hope-Filled Anthem for the Woman Who Feels She is Both Too Much and Never Enough By Hayley Morgan and Jess Connolly
Grace for the Good Girl: Letting Go of the Try-Hard Life By Emily Freeman
Uninvited: Living Loved When You Feel Less Than, Left Out, and Lonely By Lysa TerKeurst

Gratitude

One Thousand Gifts: A Dare to Live Fully Right Where You Are By Ann Voskamp

Guide to Life

Notes from a Blue Bike: The Art of Living Intentionally in a Chaotic World By Tsh Oxenreider
Boundaries: When to Say YES, When to Say NO, To Take Control of Your Life By Dr. Henry Cloud and Dr. John Townsend
Hands Free Life: Nine Habits for Overcoming Distraction, Living Better, and Loving More By Rachel Macy Stafford
For the Love: Fighting for Grace in a World of Impossible Standards By Jen Hatmaker
Freefall to Fly: A Breathtaking Journey Toward a Life of Meaning By Rebekah Lyons
The Finishing School: How One Book Nerd Began Living What She Learned By Valerie Woerner

Biblical Womanhood

Jesus Feminist: An Invitation to Revisit the Bible's View of Women By Sarah Bessey
Giddy Up Eunice: Because Women Need Each Other By Sophie Hudson

Marriage

A God-Sized Love Story: Beautiful Redemption from Beginning to End By Gretchen Saffles

Sacred Marriage: What If God Designed Marriage to Make Us Holy More Than to Make Us Happy? By Gary Thomas
What Every Bride Needs to Know: The Most Important Year in a Woman's Life By Susan DeVries and Bobbie Wolgemuth
The Antelope in the Living Room: The Real Story of Two People Sharing One Life By Melanie Shankle

Dating

How to Get a Date Worth Keeping: Be Dating in Six Months or Your Money Back By Dr. Henry Cloud and Dr. John Townsend
Boundaries in Dating: How Healthy Choices Grow Healthy Relationships By Dr. Henry Cloud and Dr. John Townsend

Memoirs and Christian Living

Cold Tangerines: Celebrating the Extraordinary Nature of Everyday Life By Shauna Niequist
Bittersweet: Thoughts on Change, Grace, and Learning the Hard Way By Shauna Niequist
Bread and Wine: A Love Letter to Life Around the Table with Recipes By Shauna Niequist
Present Over Perfect: Leaving Behind Frantic for a Simpler, More Soulful Way of Living By Shauna Niequist
Let's All Be Brave: Living Life with Everything You Have By Annie F. Downs
Looking for Lovely: Collecting the Moments that Matter By Annie F. Downs
7: An Experimental Mutiny Against Excess By Jen Hatmaker
Anything: The Prayer That Unlocked My God and My Soul By Jennie Allen
Nobody's Cuter Than You: A Memoir about the Beauty of Friendship By Melanie Shankle
Sparkly Green Earrings: Catching the Light at Every Turn By Melanie Shankle

Using Your Gifts

A Million Little Ways: Uncover the Art You Were Made to Live By Emily Freeman
Rhinestone Jesus: Saying Yes to God When Sparkly, Safe Faith Is No Longer Enough By Kristen Welch
Undaunted: Daring to do what God has called you to By Christine Caine

Biblical Truths

Steadfast Love: The Response of God to the Cries of Our Heart By Lauren Chandler
Redeeming Love By Francine Rivers
God Is Able By Priscilla Shirer
Unashamed: Drop the Baggage, Pick up Your Freedom, Fulfill Your Destiny By Christine Caine

Made in the USA
Middletown, DE
05 October 2018